©1993 Watts Books

Watts Books
96 Leonard Street
London
EC2A 4RH

Franklin Watts Australia
14 Mars Road
Lane Cove
NSW 2066

UK ISBN: 0 7496 1198 7

Dewey Decimal Classification Number 594

10 9 8 7 6 5 4 3 2 1

A CIP catalogue record for this book is available from the British Library.

Editor: Sarah Ridley
Designer: Janet Watson
Picture researcher: Sarah Moule
Illustrator: Angela Owen

Photographs: Bruce Coleman Ltd 7, 10, 15, 27; Frank Lane Picture Agency 18; Natural History Photographic Agency cover, 24; Planet Earth Pictures 8, 13, 16, 21, 23.

Printed in Malaysia

## LIFT OFF!

# MOLLUSCS

Joy Richardson

**WATTS BOOKS**
London • New York • Sydney

# Molluscs since the dinosaurs

Snails and slugs,
oysters and limpets,
squids and octopuses
are all molluscs.

Molluscs have a soft body
and most of them have a shell.

The first molluscs lived in the sea
many millions of years before
dinosaurs roamed the earth.

Mollusc shells from long ago
can be found as fossils
embedded in the rock.

# Boneless bodies

Molluscs do not have bones inside them.

Mollusc bodies are squashy and stretchy.
The main working parts are
in a hump covered by a layer
of flesh, called the mantle.
This hump contains the heart,
the stomach and the intestines.

Molluscs do not have a hard head.
Slugs can stretch out their tentacles
with eyes on the end,
or pull their head right in.

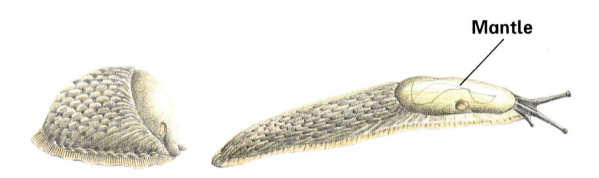

Mantle

# Starting life

Molluscs grow from eggs.

Some molluscs lay eggs which float on the water like tiny bubbles. Some molluscs fasten their eggs to stones or seaweed.

Sea slugs lay their eggs in ribbons of jelly.

Some snail eggs grow into tiny animals inside the parent's body.

Whelks lay their eggs in clusters. The empty egg cases look like sponges washed up on the beach.

# Growing a shell

Most molluscs have a shell
to protect their soft body.

The shell grows from the mantle
around the mollusc's hump.

The mantle makes a chalky liquid
which hardens into shell.

As the mollusc grows, new rings
or twists are added to the shell.

The mollusc never grows out of its shell.
The shell keeps growing with it.

# Molluscs with big feet

A snail lives inside a shell
that coils round in a spiral.
You can see the little point
where the shell started growing.

Snails have a big foot for moving.
The foot makes slime which helps
the snail to slide over the ground.

Muscles like ropes can pull the
foot back into the snail's shell.

The snail can close off the shell opening
with a layer of slime.
This helps to stick the snail down and
stops the snail from drying out.

# Sea snails

Empty shells are washed up on beaches when the molluscs inside have died.

The spiral shells belonged to different types of sea snail, such as whelks and winkles.

The whelk stretches out a big foot and crawls through the muddy sand. It attacks other creatures with a tongue covered in tiny teeth like a saw.

It pushes up a tube to bring clean water into its hump. Gills in the hump collect oxygen from the water to keep the whelk alive.

# A place on the rocks

Limpets cling to rocks
when the tide goes out.

The big foot clamps down
like a sucker and the
cone shell closes over it.

When the tide comes in,
the limpet lifts its shell lid
and moves around on its foot.
It scrapes seaweed from the rocks
with its long rasping tongue.

Then it returns to anchor itself
again in exactly the same place.

# Buried in the sand

Some molluscs have double shells with a hinge to open them.

Razor shells live in the sand. The foot pokes out of one end, burrows in the sand and pulls the shell down after it.

The razor shell does not go looking for food. It sticks two tubes up above the sand. One tube lets water into the hump. Little bits of food are collected from the water which is then pumped out of the other tube.

Cockles, mussels, scallops and oysters all have hinged shells.

Mussels tie themselves down and stay in one place.
Their foot produces a thick liquid which hardens into strong white threads.

Scallops can swim.
They flap their shells
to squirt out water
and push themselves along.
They have lots of eyes for keeping a look-out all around.

**Cockle**

**Mussel**

**Oyster**

# Slugs

Slugs are big-footed, like snails, but they have no shell.

Land slugs are dark and plain. They taste nasty so nothing tries to eat them.

Sea slugs are better looking. They may be brightly coloured or covered in feathery tufts. Their vivid patterns warn enemies to keep away. Sea slugs can sting.

# Octopus and squid

The octopus has powerful eyesight
and a good brain, but it has no head.

All its body parts are close together
in the hump covered by the mantle.

It has a mouth like a beak and
eight tentacles lined with suckers
for catching fish and crabs.

If it is in danger, it squirts
out a cloud of ink to hide itself.

The squid is a relation
of the octopus.
The giant squid is
the biggest mollusc of all.

# Mollusc facts

Molluscs have a soft body with no skeleton inside. Most live in water.

Some molluscs breathe air. Most have gills to collect oxygen from the water.

Some molluscs hunt for food. Some take it from the water which flows through their body.

Most molluscs have a shell. The shell often lasts longer than the mollusc inside it.

# Index

Body 6, 9, 11, 12, 26, 28

Cockle 22

Egg 11

Fossils 6
Foot 14, 17, 19, 20, 22, 25

Gills 17, 28

Head 9
Hump 9, 12, 17, 20, 26

Limpet 6, 19

Mantle 9, 12, 26
Mollusc 6, 9, 11, 12, 14, 17, 20, 26, 28
Muscle 14
Mussel 22

Octopus 6, 26
Oyster 6, 22

Razor shell 20

Scallop 22
Sea slug 11, 25
Sea snail 17
Shell 6, 12, 14, 17, 19, 20, 22, 25, 28
Slug 6, 9, 25
Snail 6, 11, 14, 25
Squid 6, 26

Tentacle 9, 26

Whelk 11, 17
Winkle 17